Food

La nourriture

lah nooreet-*yoor*

Illustrated by Clare Beaton

Illustré par Clare Beaton

b small publishing

bread

le pain

ler pah

fruit

les fruits

leh *froo*-ee

egg

l'œuf

lerf

cheese

le fromage

ler fro*mash*

ice cream

la glace

lah glas

fruit juice

le jus de fruit

ler shoo der *froo*-ee

cake

le gâteau

ler gat-*oh*

chicken

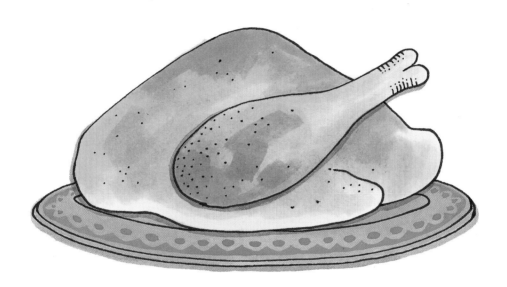

le poulet

ler poo-*leh*

biscuit

le biscuit

ler beesk-*wee*

ham

le jambon

ler shom-*bon*

milk

le lait

ler leh

A simple guide to pronouncing the French words

- Read this guide as naturally as possible, as if it were standard British English.
- Put stress on the letters in *italics* e.g. ler gat*oh*
- Don't roll the r at the end of the word, e.g. in the French word le (the): ler.

la nourriture	lah nooreet-*yoor*	**food**
le pain	ler pah	**bread**
les fruits	leh *froo*-ee	**fruit**
l'œuf	lerf	**egg**
le fromage	ler from*ash*	**cheese**
la glace	lah glas	**ice cream**
le jus de fruit	ler shoo der *froo*-ee	**fruit juice**
le gâteau	ler gat-*oh*	**cake**
le poulet	ler poo-*leh*	**chicken**
le biscuit	ler beesk-*wee*	**biscuit**
le jambon	ler shom-*bon*	**ham**
le lait	ler leh	**milk**

Published by b small publishing
The Book Shed, 36 Leyborne Park, Kew, Richmond, Surrey, TW9 3HA, UK
www.bsmall.co.uk
© b small publishing, 2003 and 2008 (new cover)
2 3 4
All rights reserved.
Printed in China by WKT Company Ltd.
ISBN-13: 978-1-902915-92-0 (UK paperback)
Cataloguing-in-Publication Data:
A catalogue record for this book is available from the British Library